Beautiful

IN ITS

Time

Finding My True Identity

STAR ANTOINETTE

◆ FriesenPress

One Printers Way
Altona, MB R0G 0B0
Canada

www.friesenpress.com

ISBN
978-1-03-917494-8 (Hardcover)
978-1-03-917493-1 (Paperback)
978-1-03-917495-5 (eBook)

1. POETRY, SUBJECTS & THEMES, INSPIRATIONAL & RELIGIOUS

Distributed to the trade by The Ingram Book Company

Life is like seasons passing through time—temporal, but all working together for a purpose. Never give up. No matter what season you find yourself in, keep looking ahead. Better things are yet to come.

Table of Contents

Introduction

Despite What You Go Through

Despite what we might go through in this life,
"He has made everything beautiful in its time"
(Ecclesiastes 3:11, New International Version [NIV]).

We go through different seasons in our lives; some are mountaintop and others are valley moments. Mountaintop moments occur when we feel elevated, joyful, and on fire because everything is working out for us. Conversely, valley moments occur when we feel like nothing is working out. We find ourselves feeling like we are at a low point in some or all areas of our lives: our mind, body, spirit, emotions, relationships, and (or) circumstances. However, it is through all these moments (the highs and the lows), that I believe God works on us the most, pushing us towards a bigger picture, as those experiences pave the way to purpose.

Beautiful in its time is a poetic expression that illustrates pivotal moments in my life journey. It describes my struggle with depression at a young age, to learning what true love is and discovering my identity as a young woman. During the past two years of the pandemic, I have found myself in what I would call a "wilderness period"—the term referring to Jesus' time in the wilderness.

Most of this book documents this period of my life, a period of isolation, growth, discovery, trials, and transformation. What I have learned from this experience is that no matter where we find ourselves in life, there is purpose in all things, even pain. Having hope that better moments are to come will keep us going. A flower or butterfly does not just obtain beauty; each, like everything in life, goes through a process, and it is through that process that their beauty develops and blossom. I believe that the poems and stories—strung throughout this book—will be relatable, bringing encouragement to you, in whatever season of life you find yourself.

STAR ANTOINETTE

A Place Called Faith

Falling light as air

With grace

Our

Worries

Being

Swept   a   w   a   y

To a place

That I call **Faith**

PART ONE

Why Can't I Be Happy? My Struggles with Depression

Save Me

Struggling for so long
This disease
Staying hidden in my blood
Recurring
Like a distant dream
Happiness seemed to flee
From my outstretched arms
As I tried to bring it close to me
Not being able to grasp it
To get rid of this disease
Yet, it remained
The enemy had thought he'd won
Trying to project his own pain
Of rejection because he did not belong
But the truth is . . .
I have been accepted and redeemed all along
On the cross of Calvary
Where my name has been called
There is a blood that washes it all
That has saved me and set me free
From depression
That has made many fall

The Spirit of Depression

People say that depression is a sickness, and it is, but it is also a spirit. It is a destructive spirit aimed to kill, steal, and destroy people's destinies. I first struggled with depression at the tender age of thirteen and did not overcome it until my early adulthood. It was like a disease that stayed dormant for a period but would flare up once triggered. I did not know what caused it, but there were a series of experiences in my life that left negative impressions on me. The only way to release these negative feelings was on paper. My pain and memories stayed locked in a black journal with a red heart, becoming a distant reality, until one day, in my older age, I found that journal. I never knew how angry and lost I was until reading that old journal, and it moved me to tears because I felt sorry for the hurt girl in between the pages. She felt neglected and bitter from her circumstances at the time, which led her to self-medicate and almost overdose when she felt tired of her life. Nobody would miss her, she convinced herself, as she felt so alone, unloved, and unworthy of life. The enemy whispered these very lies to poison her mind. These lies were projections that came from the devil and were received by whoever accepted them. If it were not for the fear of God that entered her heart in that split second, the day those half blue and white pills filled the palm of her hand, she would not be here to tell you her story; she would just be another destiny taken by this violent disease.

I Sink Deep

....

Treading slowly
Led limbs
Water creeps up
Needles prick my skin
My throat
Suffocating me

I sink deep

Abyss
Time
Goes on
Pulling
Me
Down
Until
I am

Nothing
I rise
Faster lighter
Water grazes my skin
Like smooth silk
Brushing against my face
Loving hands pulling me up
Eyes slowly open
To a warm light
Free
I rise

God Turned My Darkness into Light

(Psalm 18:28)

I was in darkness, about to drown, until a hand reached out from above and pulled me out of deep waters (Psalm 18:16). Reading that old journal made me realize how much God had turned my life around. It amazed me to see the difference between the little girl inside the journal and the woman outside it. Back then, I did not know God, even though I grew up in church. God to me seemed like a far-away, divine being who did not have any time for me, and so I did not have any time for Him, either. Yet, no matter how many remedies I tried to numb my pain, the only remedy that I later found to work was Jesus. I believed in God before, but it was not until I had my first encounter with Christ that I decided to surrender my life to Him. My encounter happened in the summer of 2020 while I was taking a nap on my mother's bed. While napping, I felt a hand holding mine. Instead of the darkness we usually see when we close our eyes, I saw all white, and kept hearing this song my mom used to sing: "Hand in hand we walk each day, hand in hand along the way, walk with God you shall not fail, hand in hand with Jesus." In this precious moment, I knew that Jesus was telling me that he was with me and to take it one step at a time because, with him, I would not fail.

Forgiveness

Weighing me down by its chains
Un-forgiveness bound me in
I tried to fly but my wings were clipped
I tried to grow but your roots tighten their grip
Refusing to let air pass through
Or sunlight to nourish
The seed yearning to produce a fruit
Needing to be freed
I had to release you from me
Doing it for me and not for you
For I am called to do greater things

It Is a Beautiful Thing

I had a dream, January 22, 2019, that was life changing. The overall understanding that I got from the dream was that I could not grow because my heart was heavy, and the source of that heaviness was my ex- "stepdad." After the dream, I spoke to my mom who told me that God was showing me that I needed to forgive my stepdad for the past hurt that he caused to move on. Although my mom and ex-stepdad were not together at that time, she encouraged me to send him an email. At the end of that email I wrote, "Forgiveness is such a beautiful thing; it will set you free," and, soon after that, I felt the same freedom of forgiveness. But it did not end with him; I had to go through a long process of forgiveness before I could work on healing the open wounds of my past.

A lot of people are bound by the chains of un-forgiveness. This is how the enemy gains access into our lives. The devil does not want us to forgive because un-forgiveness can cost us heaven. If we cannot forgive one another then how can we expect God to forgive us? It can also be a hindrance in our lives, as it becomes a stumbling block to our growth. Forgiveness is about the posture of the heart. If your heart is weighed down with anger, resentment, and bitterness, it will be hard to make room for anything else. Bitterness took up most of the room in my heart, and because of that, my heart was closed off, and I felt incapable of expressing love. Un-forgiveness can also take away your peace and joy. Forgiveness is not for the other person but it is for you, and the words "I forgive you" hold so much power that it releases us from the bondages of un-forgiveness; however, it needs to be done truly from our hearts. You will know when you truly forgive someone when you see their face, hear their voice or name, and it does not cause a negative reaction in you. I know that forgiveness is hard, but I want to encourage anyone who is struggling to forgive, to take that leap of faith like I did, and to release it. If you want to move on and grow, then it is time to let go.

Haiku Poems

Feelings

Feelings like seasons
Change in the movements of time
Unreal in my mind

Paid It All

Depression is debt
Coming to collect in death
But Christ paid it all

Set Free

Ready to fly free
From the bondage of sin
Above the limitless sky

Overcoming Negative Emotions

I used to be ruled by my emotions to the point where I would welcome the numbness that would sometimes come along. My emotions governed how I would perceive the world and the things happening around me. Often, they gave me wrong impressions, making things look worse. That is how I would get sucked into the rabbit hole of depression, by misinterpreting perceptions that would trigger harmful emotions that sometimes made me feel like I was dying inside. I had to learn to take control of my thoughts, and to check myself by questioning if I was processing things correctly. I would ask myself, Am I perceiving this right? Where are these emotions coming from? Why did this trigger my sadness? Once I was able to get them in check, I learned how to not be enslaved by my feelings but to rise above them. How did I do this? I had to learn that even though my emotions were very much felt and real to me, they were temporal and unstable feelings based on lies about myself and things going on around me.

When we have negative emotions and thoughts about ourselves, we need to identify the source of them. God did not create us with negative emotions and thoughts; they are unnatural. They are called lies because they are not our reality. Everything that God created was and is good, but bad thoughts are destructive. All that opposes the good that God created comes from the enemy and knowing this truth can help us combat these negative thoughts. This is also why in Romans 12 it is encouraged for us to renew our minds and not to conform to the ways and mindset of this world. We also need to know who we are in Christ. How do we get to know ourselves? We get to know ourselves through the Word of God and having it dwelling in us. We need to be filled with the Spirit of God because, when we are, we gain the fruits, which are joy, peace, love, and much more. Lastly, we need to pray for stability in our emotions and pray for it daily.

Temptation

The man behind the tree offers a fruit   the shininess of the apple
reflecting the whiteness of his suit   but the fruit is rotten from the inside
as he feeds me lies   his lips twist into an unusual smilehissing into my
ear as a snake tries to talk but on the right stands a lion   and it fights
with the man and the snake   behind the safety of my mind   the war
goes on as I continue to smile

. . .

Mind-War

It is so easy to wear a mask, but even that mask can crack after a
while, showing that it was not perfect all along
(Star Antoinette).

So many people are at war within their minds. Our minds are the first place
that gets attacked, because our minds are a powerful driving force to the
outcome of our lives. My mind was always being attacked by lies and negative
perceptions, and the temptation to accept them, which can lead to grave con-
sequences. Accepting lies tempts us to give up on our dreams, gifts, ourselves,
and even others.

When it comes to battling undesirable thoughts or other struggles we face
mentally, a lot of us tend to stay silent. I always hid the struggles that went
on in my mind and pretended like I was fine, but the more I kept it in, the
more it started to show. I had to learn to cast down these lies and imaginations,
while making a conscious decision to stop dwelling on them, combating them
with positivity instead. We must break the stigma surrounding mental health,
which can become a silent killer when we internalize our struggles and do not
speak out or do anything to get help for fear of condemnation.

Insanity

Help me to overcome
This torrent of feelings coming undone
Renew my mind in your Word
From this world I have become
Threatening to destroy me
As I stand on the brink of insanity

Combating Lies with the Truth of God's Words

....

I still struggle, at times, with negative thoughts and feelings as a Christian, but the difference between then and now is that they no longer rule me, and I know, if I stay in the Word of God, they never will again. It is all right not to always be okay, as long as we do not stay in those feelings and let them rule us. We must create positive space for our emotions, which are a part of our human experience. However, our emotions are unstable, as they can change in an instant. Knowing that they are temporary and that we will go through them can help us not to be buried by them. At one point, I could not trust myself or what I felt because my emotions were so unstable. I had to find refuge somewhere, and I found it in the comforting, stable Word of God. This was big—coming from a person who never desired to pick up her bible before, and when she did, she either read it with a lack of understanding or fell asleep. One thing that stood out for me about the Word of God was that it said, in Matthew 24:35, "Heaven and earth will pass away, but my Words will never pass away." Everything is always changing in this world, even our emotions. I needed the stable Word of God to help me fight the negative lies that flooded my mind, trying to destroy me.

Under My Feet

Crushed by the heaviness of grief
Crackling sounds fill the silence
Threatening to burst at the seams
Creating jagged lines in my heartbeat
Pounding uncontrollably

Crying out in the stillness, my contrite spirit
Unaware that you are near to the broken-hearted
You try to reach out to me
The thickness of my worries drowns you out
Making it hard to see
Past the things that are temporary in this moment of grief

Looking up to the heavens
For answers
Radiant light kisses my cheek
Reversing the weight of gravity
You help me to stand
As I trample fear under my feet

He Understands

It can be hard to see any light when we are so lost in grief, which can be suffocating because it consumes all our attention. It leaves us feeling like there is not only no way out but also no way in for anyone to reach us. In these moments in which I found myself in a dark pit, I felt alone; I could not feel God's presence, hear His voice, or see any form of light in my circumstances. But, through the past couple of years of this pandemic, I have experienced God in those dark moments. In Psalm 34, it says that the Lord draws close to the broken-hearted and those crushed in their spirit. I have discovered that God is not far away but right here with us if we allow Him. We do not have to be perfect in approaching Him. I cannot tell you how many times I have come to God completely broken not knowing what to say, as I have cried, screamed, or even just sat in silence. In Hebrews 4:15, it says that Jesus empathizes with our weaknesses because He experienced temptation, too, but the only difference is that it did not lead Him to sin. He understands what we go through and knows that we are not always going to be strong; we can lean on Him for strength and comfort in our time of need.

Perfect

Filled to the brim
Ready to spill over
These tears I am trying to hold in
My elastic grin
Stretching uncomfortably across my skin
Close to snapping
It hides in the forced, "I'm okay"
But, I can't fake it with you
You see from within
The burdens of my heart
You tell me to pour it out
To cast my burdens
Giving me your shoulder to cry on
Letting go of all control
I fall back into your loving arms
Finally, at rest
Not having to be perfect

It's Okay to Not Be Okay

....

"Casting all your anxiety on him because he cares for you"
(1 Peter 5:7).

I whispered this scripture many times when the weight of my worries was bearing down on my shoulders. The heavy load of uneasiness was something I have felt for so long that my bones started to cry out for rest. I was tired of trying to be alright; even after these past couple of years of the world turning upside down, I was done pretending. It was more exhausting to act like I was fine. So, one morning, I set all pretense aside and really broke down. I was so full of anxiety about where my life was going, I started to cry while a song flowed from the depths of my distress. The little night gown I wore was drenched in sweat; my face was sticky with my tears. I sung about surrendering my life, as I let go of trying to be perfect that morning and told the Lord, "Here is my life; I do not know what I am doing, so I surrender it to you." Then, the Spirit of the Lord took over and I could feel in my heart the Lord saying everything would be okay.

In Your Fullness of Joy

My Joy comes to me
Like crashing waves
Going in and out, in and out
I want it to stay
But the currents always sweep it away
Cradling it in the cups of my hands
But no matter how careful
It drains through the cracks of my fingers
Trickling down slowly to go back to sea
Then it's gone again . . .

Oh Lord, fill me with your fullness of joy
Make my cup overflow
With abundance that will never run short
Let it wash over me like a protective layer
Seeping into my skin
Becoming a part of me
Let it dance with me at dawn
Filling the air with laughter
Let it wrap its arms around
And cover me from the raging storm
Let it shield me from its cold currents
Biting the tips of my toes
Leaving behind grains of salt like streaks of tears . . .
I don't want to be alone
Let it shield me from the burning rays
Of the sun rising over the waters
Let its power resonate
Making the waves die down as stillness comes
In your quiet presence
Filling me with your fullness of joy

Waves of Happiness

"My joy comes to me like crashing waves," is an observation I made one day after I woke up and asked God a serious question or two: "Why could my joy not stay? Why did it come to me like waves that came and went?" Then, my eyes opened to see the reason why my joy could not be constant, and it was because my joy was rooted in my circumstances. A lot of us struggle with this problem because we tend to put our joy in our jobs, people, substances, and other things. However, we cannot put our happiness in these temporal things because they are constantly changing, as life is filled with ups, downs, and surprising turns.

Each of us has a choice in everything we do in life and that also includes our emotions, which can frame the outcome of the way we choose to live each day. The decision to choose joy was not easy, but I had to make the conscious decision to choose it and to renew my mind. It has always been a constant battle for me to remain joyful, but I have come to realize that it is a choice and one that we must make daily. What I did to help me choose joy daily was read the Word of God, speak it until I believed it, stopped trying to control everything, forgive myself and others, and change my mindset and perspective. There is no true joy outside of Christ, and that is something I realized living in a world full of pain and suffering. Life and joy are on the other side of depression, and the truth is we are not alone. We are loved beyond measure and filled with purpose; our lives are precious to God.

PART TWO

What Is Love?
Relearning What Love Is
and What It Looks Like

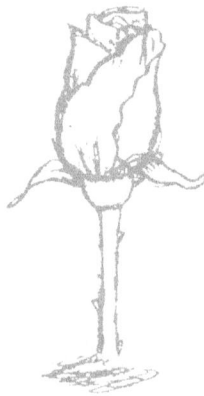

20

Relearning

I have always wondered what falling in love felt like and how I would react when I finally found it. I imagined it would be like how my stomach felt at the big drop of a roller coaster or when a wave came rushing at you all at once, overwhelming you until you gasped for air. The only reference I had about falling in love was from the romantic movies and books I would watch and read. I never thought that knowing God's love could improve connections romantically because it was something I never saw growing up. I grew up seeing fighting and no peace, disrespect, and no honour, instability, and no true commitment. As a result, I had made a promise to myself to never have a relationship like that and to wait. But, in my young age and pre-mature relationship with God, the "determination" of waiting for genuine love turned to bitterness, distrust, and fear towards men. These feelings took a toll on me, as I started to accept a lie that I did not deserve love or was incapable of having the love that I so desired to experience. This led me to make the wrong choice in my first relationship, so, I made a vow not to date again; if I did, the next man would be my husband. Without consciously knowing what this vow meant, I gave my love life to God, allowing him to be the author of that story. I had to unlearn the love of this world and the one I saw in my childhood and relearn love from a Godly perspective.

No Greater Love

They say your love is the greatest
An extension of the divine
Sweeping throughout the nations
Surpassing understanding of mankind
It does not run out of patience
Nor run out of time
Leaving the ninety-nine
To go after the lost one
It leaves no one behind

They say your love is the greatest
A mender of broken hearts
Restoring and healing
In Christ, giving us a new start
Your grace revealing
How unmerited and unconditional it is
To be loved by you
The thought of it like a sweetened kiss
Oh, I don't deserve it
But you call me your own
A bridegroom coming back for his bride
Only to you I belong

They say your love is the greatest
Because you gave your life for mine
So, teach me to love
Like that great love of the divine

Unconditional:
Understanding God as a Father

I never had a good male role model growing up to show me love. I was raised by a hard-working single mother who played both roles of a parent to me. The lack of an active Father in my life made it hard to understand that God, as the Father, loved me deeply and so much that nothing could even separate me from His love as said in Romans 8. When I started to learn about God's love, I saw how unconditional it was because God chose to love us even when we were deep in our sins. He chased us even when we chose to run away. He chose to accept us even when we rejected Him. It hit me that love was a choice, and despite what we do, Jesus still chooses to love us. His love is the mandate of how we should love one another; the first commandment is to love thy God with all our heart, mind, and strength, and then to love others. When we know God's love, then we will learn how to truly love one another. Understanding God's love, helped me to forgive, let go of resentment and love my biological father later when we were reconciling our relationship. God's love sets us free and tells us we are enough. In 1 Corinthians 13 it says, if we do not have love, we have nothing. His love taught me that I am seen, heard, deeply loved, and known by Him, and that I belong and deserve to be loved. God's love is something I had to learn and still learning through my own journey.

Two Are Better than One

Wrapped in your arms
I cling to you like a starving child
Abiding in the heavens above . . .

I need more of you

You said two are better than one
So let us become one
One body
One mind
One soul
One spirit
One heartbeat
Binding with your covenant
Strung together by a three-headed cord
No one can break up what you put together
No one can separate us from your love

Made for Love

We were made to love and be loved, which is why we crave companionship and fellowship. From the beginning of time, God said it was not good for man to be alone and made Eve, a helpmate for Adam. I longed for that companionship, to experience God's love in a relationship because I was so tired of seeing the relationships around me end up in shambles. I, myself, was also weary of relationships ending badly, whether they were friendships or romantic. The heartache, difficulties, and sin of my past relationship helped me realize that when God is at the centre of our relationships, they will not fail, no matter what life throws at us. When we build our relationships on a solid foundation, they can withstand any storm.

Don't Silence My "No"

When did my no become a challenge—
Or a flirt or a right of passage for you to invade my space?
When did the repetition of it become a repeated offence—
The strength behind it disappearing with every
No, No, no, no . . .
Until my no became unsure—
Changing to maybes and then silence
Worn down by the constant persistence of its perpetrator
Forcing himself in
Stripping me bare
Until I am suddenly exposed
Because my no could not protect me anymore?
When did it stop mattering?

The Power of the Word No

No is such a powerful word, but when it is taking away from you, it can lead you into a pit, which is what happened to me in my first relationship. I was so desperate to experience love that I ignored the red flags. In my attempt to keep that love, I tolerated a lot just to appease the person I was with at the time. Saying yes when I really wanted to say no or my no turning into a yes after being worn down by a persistent "please" or "this is how we show we love each other." My wavering no came with consequences that left me feeling empty every time. I experienced a mental breakdown at one point, and after that, decided not to give my body away just to feel loved. Unfortunately, that would not be the last time my no would not be respected. From having a trusted male-friend trying to force himself on me, to being cornered in a dark space of a club forced to kiss a guy who refused to move unless I kissed him, my noes were overlooked and left me feeling unsafe. I wanted to experience a pure love that created a safe place for me. Every person has their own definition of what love is, but the true definition comes out of the Word of God. If your no is not being respected, then it is a sign to walk away from that toxic relationship. I told myself that if I were to let down my walls and love again, I wanted someone with good character who would respect my boundaries, my body, and my no.

Out of Reach

White dress flowing down past the knees
Puddling at the feet
Trailing behind like fallen leaves
Making a pathway up to a special place
The beautiful altar
Where God and beloved awaits the bride to be
That is what I saw
But never did I think it could be me
It was so far out of reach
As a young girl I started to believe that I didn't deserve love

Until you showed up, a love like no other
So vast and free, surpassing the stars and moon
Unlimited like the universe
Deeper than the ocean and long like eternity
A love so kind, gentle, and true
You said, I am worthy of being pursued

Least when I expected, your love came through like a soft whisper
Slipping past the walls of my heart
And making room as I slowly opened up
Unravelling like a flower about to bloom
Pollinated by your love that was birthing something new

Dreams of a bride finally meeting her bridegroom
Dances on the whimsical promises spoken in the midnight hour
Too soon, being whisked away again out of reach
As the season changes, bittersweet
But, still hopeful of that love returning to me

The Vision

There are two things I always wanted to believe in but didn't dare.
One is that there was one man, somewhere, who was made just for
me. The other is that I just might deserve him
(*Still Breathing* [movie]).

"There is no such thing as love." This lie crept into my mind in my early 20s. I did not believe in "soulmates" either, and I started to accept that marriage was not for me. The idea of love, marriage, and happiness with someone was like a distant dream. Until one day in 2020, I got a vision from God. This vision sparked a passion in me. It dared me to believe that there was a man out there for me and that marriage was a part of God's plan for me. In that vision, I received a package and in that package was two extra things I was not expecting and one of them was a shirt that said "bride." After that vision, I started to have dreams about a man I did not know but felt a deep love for, and it was mutual. I did not know when or where I would meet this man, but he felt very much real to me, so, I decided to wait for him no matter how long it took because I was done settling. I wanted the best; I dared to believe that I deserved it. The Lord also said that because I waited, I would get the best. I held onto the vision, believed in the vision, and as weird as it sounded, I fell in love with the vision. But, the vision was bittersweet, close but still out of reach.

Longing

I have yearned for your kind of love
For so long
That I have become numb
Burying the desire deep
A lost treasure
I wanted to keep
Killing the hope
Reminiscing in my dreams
But you called dead things back to life
You, the resurrected King

Let it Go

Hard to release it
I keep the promise in like a caged bird
Afraid to open the gates
And let it go
Struggling to trust your words
When you say,
Nobody can take it away
What is yours will be yours

Delayed Promises

"Hope deferred makes the heart sick" (Proverbs 13:12 [NIV]).

Yearning for that love in my dreams, my heart started to ache. Disappointment, frustration, doubt, and mistrust started to mix with the vision that God gave me. I felt like I was being teased with the promise of my soulmate. Month after month, one year and a half later, I was still single and tired of waiting. For the sake of my faith, I had to put that vision aside. I also gave up on the vision when I finally met someone that I deeply connected with but as quickly as it started, it came to a swift end. I found myself yet again alone when I realized that he was not the man for me. During this wait, I discovered that it was not God taunting me with the vision but preparing me for it. In Numbers 23:19, it says that God is not like humans, that He should lie or change His mind. His timing is not our timing, and just because it is delayed it does not mean He will not fulfill His promise.

Second Chance

We both did not know what love was
We never saw it growing up
It was like a faraway fantasy,
Some dream that was out of reach
We believed that we were undeserving of it
Of being loved simply for who we are
Not having to pretend

We craved a kind of love that was accepting
That said "I love you no matter what"
A love that never left when the going got tough
A full year-round kind of love that did not change
As the seasons did
But was constant and could not be shaken
One that remained a firm foundation

A love that loved us deeper than our sins
And did not hold us to our past
A love that is so forgiving and so full of trust
We didn't find that love but that love found us
And said that we are enough
Mending back the pieces
When we took our broken hearts to Jesus
He sewed it back together
Healing us from the hurt that threatened to pass on
To the next generation because hurt travels along

He said we were worthy of being loved
But we questioned, Who could love us in our mess?
So, we bore our guilt and shame instead
Covered in crimson red and so dirty from the past life we led
Nonetheless, you redeemed our time with the price that was paid
Giving us a second chance
A second chance at a life and love that we so prayed

Bittersweet

"I do not want to talk to any guy" is what I said to myself at a birthday party right before I met him. We were waiting to help my stepdad load things into the car when he started to talk to me. Since that night, we got very close, it seemed that the conversation was never-ending. I was surprised when I found myself connecting with this man on an emotional, intellectual, and even spiritual level. What stood out to me about him was how easy it was for us to talk. I remembered one of the many first conversations we had: we both admitted that we really did not know what love was because we never grew up seeing it. We were raised by our mothers and did not have men to teach or show us what it meant to love and be loved. We also thought we were not worthy of the love that we desired. But, when we accepted Christ's love into our lives, we started to believe that we had the capacity to recreate what we did not see growing up or experience in previous relationships. What we were not taught about love by our earthly fathers, we were being taught by our Heavenly Father. In a short span of five months, we developed a deep friendship and spiritual connection. However, we were led away by our desire to love and be loved so badly that we did not want to wait on God. I noticed that our relationship was being built on shaky grounds, which made us start to go outside of God's will for our lives. That kind of love led me astray and made me realize that it is more than just finding a Christian man and being in love but finding someone who has the same convictions in purity and purpose. This is someone whose vision for their life aligns with yours. Are they compatible? Do they truly respect your boundaries and fear God enough to protect your purity? Although our time together was short, we were taught that we deserved a chance at love and the life we desired, but at the right time and with the right person.

Love

Love is the blisters welted on the palm of your hands
As you held the weight of your death dragging behind you
Love is the insults hurled as daggers to your heart, but despite that you
kept going
Love is the sweat dripping down your neck and the stinging of the sun on
your bare back
Love is the hatred released as spit escaped their lips, disgust touching your
face, but yet you went on
Love is the scars on your back making a pattern wherever the whip landed
It's the deepest wounds that penetrated your flesh
Love is the tiny pricks from the thorns pierced in your scalp as you looked up
Saying
"Father forgive them"
Love is the last resounding words
"It is finished!"
Echoing in the still air as you took your last breath

The Cross

Jesus redefined the meaning of love and its outlook to me. The previous poem, "Love," explores the meaning of true love with nonconventional illustrations. It explores a side of love that is unappealing, as love is not always beautiful and can even be ugly at times. Sometimes, it is about suffering and sacrifice. It can also be enduring and patient. Love does not always make sense, but it is selfless. This is what real love is. It is not always pleasant. If we could just grasp this unfiltered meaning, then our relationships with one another would be different. It is undoubtable that it was not easy for Jesus to endure crucifying pain for sinners whom he loved, but it was for a bigger purpose, our salvation. In those grievous moments when Jesus was beaten, spat upon, and verbally harassed, he adamantly continued to choose us, his people, even until his last words, "It is finished." Jesus showed us that love is a choice that we constantly have to make no matter our circumstances or conditions. I am amazed with Jesus' continual tenderness towards us. Indeed, caring for those you like is effortless, but imagine the difficulty in caring for those who hate you or those whom you despise? Despite everything, Jesus told the Father in Heaven to forgive his persecutors because they did not know what they were doing. He still does this up until today, forgiving us. Jesus persisted along the arduous path to Calvary knowing full well that he was rejected by his people. That is the beauty of the cross—the display of sincere love at its rawest form.

PART THREE

Who Am I?
Finding and Learning
My Identity

Child of God

Stained in mud down to my feet
But still you chose me
Scrubbed red, you washed me clean
Clothing me in your best robe
Crowned in your majesty
Wrapped in authority
In your eyes
The finest of gems
A royal diadem in your hand
Your ruby
Shinning in your glorious light
Amongst the kings and queens
Your imperishable beauty
Empowering
As I enter the palace of the King

What Does It Mean to be a Child of God?

A part of our life assignment is to discover our purpose, but to do so, we must first uncover our identity
(Star Antoinette).

When I was younger, I never gave an intentional thought towards my identity, but I always had this feeling that I was meant to do something great. Little did I know, the feeling came from the plans that were already set for me. As I grew older, I realized that having an identity runs deeper and holds a greater importance because it is a part of our life purpose. Growing up in a Christian home, I was told that my identity was attached to being a child of God, but up until recently I never really knew what that meant. Being a child of God meant that God was my Father, and because I was His child, I was also His heir. "You are no longer a slave, but God's child; and since you are his child, God has made you also an heir" (Galatians 4:7). As an heir, we are called into a great inheritance, which is eternal life, but also to fulfill a greater purpose here on earth. When we discover and step into our identity as children of the King, the Creator of the Universe, then we can face life with confidence, boldness, and the dominion that He has given us. We all have a purpose, no matter if you believe in God or not, or what your past or present predicaments are. God made no mistake in creating us.

Mold Me

I am the clay in the potter's hands
Formless to his touch
Spinning round and round and round
As water runs over
Making something out of me
Under his care I start to move
To a rhythmic beat

Smoothing the rough edges,
Removing the parts that won't fit
Making the crooked places straight,
Showing me the way
I start to change with his simple guidance
Creating the course of my fate
Spinning round and round and round
Feeling pressure on all sides
I begin to abound
My measures expanding,
My old walls breaking down
Forming into Christ's image
As the wheel keeps spinning
Round and round and round
In the potter's hands

Uncovering

Not fully understanding who I am was like walking with a veil over my eyes. I imagined this was what a bride felt like on her wedding day—her veil covering her face as she navigated her way down the aisle. Feeling slightly disoriented, her only guide being the gentle arm looped around hers. Trusting that it would lead her to the altar where the groom would remove the veil, allowing her to finally see clearly. The aisle was life, and the altar was the divine moment of discovering one's identity; the groom to unveil it to me was Jesus. Most of us walk through life blindly not knowing who we are and why we are here, but we have a sense that there is something bigger than us. We are like that bride: our eyes are closed off from seeing our lives clearly. Then there are those who allow themselves to be guided through the blindness to that unveiling—the moment when it all becomes crystal clear and suddenly you know. Not all of us are fortunate to reach that moment of epiphany or encounter in our lives, and should strive to reach it by seeking the One who can reveal it to us. You will find me when you search for me with all your heart (Jeremiah 29:13).

Figurines

Pristine glass of figurines
Stand on a wooden desk
Dull
Your distorted reflection
Curved in the shapes
That clouds the eyes looking away
Tipping over the edge
Pristine glass—
Shattered like crystals
Glistening, across the floor
Your clear face
Reflected in the jagged pieces
Sharpened the eyes looking back

Light of the World

We are called the light of the world in Matthew 5:14, but we cannot be the light if we do not know who we are and whose we are. Instead of shinning, we become dull. Blinded by unrealistic expectations and flashy trends that makes it hard for us to see ourselves the way God sees us. As I have mentioned, Romans 12:2 of the bible tells us not to conform to this world but to be transformed by the renewing of our mind. We renew our mind in God's word, which is a transforming agent that helps us discover ourselves, as it breaks those negative views and false truths in our culture. We were made in God's image, which means we are supposed to have the characteristics of His Spirit: love, joy, peace, patience, faithfulness, self-control, long suffering, and kindness. However, in this world, we are left with hate, depression, worries/anxiety, impatience, distrust, self-gratification, quick fixes, and indecencies. We are taught to self-hate or compare ourselves because we are never fully satisfied. Breaking the figurines is being free of worldly expectations and seeing who we truly are in Christ. We are meant to shine, to stand out; we are meant to be who God has formed and called us to be from the beginning of time; we are meant to fulfill our purpose and reach our full potentials.

Colour

Splinters of wood pierce the bottom of my feet   as an open door
creaks   there I stood   the centre of a crowd   dark eyes burning like fire
scorching my skin   punishing me   like I have sinned   standing there
with nothing to say   in a gloomy white room   I am the cracks in between
the walls   look at her hair   look at her nose   as bits of me disappear
like the brown of my skin fading into thin air   knowing that I cannot be
repaired   but I am aware of the pale girl that stands before me   similar
but easy to compare   the heads turn to her with a pleasant smile   but
turn into something vile   when they look at me all the eyes stare   as they
continue to judge the colour that I wear

STAR ANTOINETTE

The Colour of My Skin Is Not My Identity

I am a woman of colour, but it is not who I am; the colour of my skin does not define my identity. However, race has become so much a part of our individuality within western culture that it's hard to separate race from self. We say we are more than just the colour of our skin, "we all bleed red," but we have become stuck on the very thing we are trying to move beyond. It is shown in the way we speak and distinguish our race. For instance, in navigating black culture, we end up sometimes subscribing to a stereotype, or a generalization based on the colour of our skin. Although there are some similarities that individuals share within their race and culture, they do not capture the entirety of who they are, which is how we start to put one another into a certain box. We try to justify our acceptance of this racial identity by "redefining" what was once racist. But our identity is not on the surface of our skin; it is deep within and is the essence of our being, soul, spirit, and who God made us to be as His child, made in His image. Yes, the colour of our skin is something we cannot easily look past but knowing that we are not just our race will help free us all from the racial chains that have plagued our society. We are spiritual beings, and racial division is what the enemy uses to cause discord and chaos, not only in the world but also sometimes even in our churches. I believe this understanding of who we really are can help us collectively overcome and conquer racism.

Where Did My Confidence Go?

Where did my confidence go?
Is she hiding somewhere behind the chair, or within the closet perhaps, or
underneath a pile of clothes?
Is she tucked under my bed, crouched beside the corner of my dresser, or
hiding behind the curtains instead?
Or did she leave this room entirely—
Slipping past the closed door
Not wanting to be seen
Not wanting to be disturbed
As I am left behind
One step closer, one step back
Not sure if I am hot or cold
I have been searching for so long . . .
Where did my confidence go?
Is she stuck in the past?
Lost within the constant fights she witnessed between two adults acting like
her, a child
Or was she overlooked, not feeling like she belonged?
As she felt like she was lacking something like a father's love
Or was she not appreciated for who she was because she was constantly
comparing herself to someone else?
Was she tossed to and fro from the lies within her mind that spoke?
Saying
You are not talented, you are not worthy, you are not pretty, you are
not enough
Where did my confidence go?
Is she aimlessly wondering around in the present—
Getting buried in the constant worry about where her life is going
Or if she is going to make it?
Caught up in the paranoid thought that everyone is judging her
Did she crumble under the pressure she put on herself?
And get swept away by the fear of failure or missed opportunities?

Or did she go on vacation because she was tired of the routine?
Where did my confidence go?
Did she dance her way to my future —
Led by the promises ahead of her?
Is she expecting me to get there so that we can finally reunite?
Or has she been patiently lingering by my side
Waiting all this time for me to embrace her?

Questions to My Confidence

Where did my confidence go? is a question that echoed through my mind. I have always struggled with my confidence, and no matter how much I tried to fake it, the absence of it would make itself known. When my lack of confidence peeked out with its ugly head, the person seeing it would let me know, and the last time it happened, it really made me start to reflect. I started asking myself questions: Is confidence something we inherently have and need to protect because there is the potential of it being lost? Or is it something we must seek out for ourselves as we go through life? If it was something we inherited, then where did mine go? When did I lose it? What happened to me along the way into adulthood that made me lack confidence? I also started to reflect on my life experiences to see if there was one or multiple events that took away my confidence. The lack of confidence could have been internal or external, but no matter what the cause was, I wanted to start focusing on rediscovering my confidence. I have been going through a process of growth, refinement, and being molded into who Star is, and I'm still getting to know her and how God sees her. I am learning to just be, being my authentic self. Being okay to be different, and not being too self-conscious, is where the confidence will come from.

Your Song

Before I came into existence you called me your song
From when I was young a melody played along . . .
Crying to be heard as purpose sung from my bones
Muffled sound trying to rise above the loud noise
You knew me before I was even formed
Ordaining me from my mother's womb
Greatness, as a Star was born
But I lost my way on that long winding road
Fear gripped my heart, discouraging me
Experiences of life encouraged me to let go
Depression tried to take me out
Leading me astray
Reckless with my life
Convincing me not to stay
To take my potential to the grave
But you fought for me and said I was worthy of being saved
Of being loved
Reaching out and rescuing me from above
You've been with me through it all
I've been through fire and did not burn
I've been through water and did not drown
But instead, I kept my faith and stood on solid ground
Trying to figure it all out now
The vision of God's plan for me
Becoming a song to the nation is what you have called me to be
To release sweet melodies and lead your people out of captivity

I Am

I am **Not,**
Stupid

I am **Not** ugly
I am **Not** weak
I am **Not** insecure
I am **Not** cursed
I am **Not** lonely
I am **No** lacking

I am **N** trapped

I am set free
I am beautiful
I am strong
I am confident
I am blessed
I am loved
I am prosperous

I am wise

Good enough
I am

Words Form Our Reality

The words we speak form our own personal reality and concept of ourselves. Life and death are in the tongue, and we need to speak the living, positive, Word of God as to who we are, to dismantle the lies and negative thoughts we tell ourselves. I had to change my language—denouncing the negative lies I spoke about myself—and start to declare who I really was. I adopted a practice of declaring these powerful affirmations over myself every morning before starting my day. Spoken words are very powerful; what we verbally proclaim will affect the way we view ourselves and the outcome of our lives, so continue to declare victory over yours.

You Chose Me

Standing on the sidelines of life
The feeling of isolation so strong
Never looking the part
Not feeling like I belonged
The last to be chosen on the team
Always feeling like a black sheep
The last to be chosen for a new opportunity
Always was my reality
The last, the last, the last
But,
How amazing is this?
The Creator of the universe
The one who saves
Who the stars and moon obey
Who shakes the mountains
And whose mighty voice moves the waves
Chose me

Belonging

Sometimes we might feel like we are standing on the sidelines of life—the last to be chosen by our teammates to play on a team or by our boss for that promotion—watching the missed opportunities that come our way. We are even the last to be picked in our friend groups, families, or by that one person we love and care for. No matter the situation or circumstance, we feel like we never get chosen.

Now, think about this . . .

The Creator of the universe, the one who created the moon and the stars, the voice that moves the mighty waves, has chosen you. How amazing is this? While others might have rejected and overlooked us, there is a love that is so big and deep that has chosen us and will keep choosing us for the rest of our days.

Called

Called to be yours from the beginning of time
Since creation
Carefully stitched into fine lines
Called to be the daughter of the King
Handpicked from the divine
Eternity with you, greater than a lifetime
Called to be your Star
I am ready to shine
Your sweet songbird
Ready to fly
Called to be bold
Mounting up like an eagle to the sky
Ahead of me, my purpose awaits
As I soar high
Counting down the days
Praying revival is on its way
Called to be your vessel
To share your light with the lost world
Your glory
Manifesting the power of your living Word
As I continue to share my story

He has saved us and called us to a holy life—not because of anything we have done but because of His own purpose and grace (2 Timothy 1:10).

PART FOUR

In The Valley
My Wilderness Period

Still Voice

....

Voices swarming like bees
Their words stinging my ears
Pulling me in all directions
I cannot hear
Yet, unconstrained
Piercing through all the noise
You said your sheep shall know you
Your still, small voice

Wilderness

Lost in the evergreen
Branches hang low
Holding me captive
Water escaping these sunken leaves
Rolling down to the ground
This isolation brought so much pain out of me
Fertilizing the soil caught in the rain
In this season, you said I have so much to gain
Sowing seeds, hoping it is joy I reap
Breaking me down to build me up
Feeling at my worst
I cry out in my waiting
Temptation lingering on the outskirts
As I find myself
Stuck in this wilderness

A Time of Isolation

The wilderness is a time of isolation. In this isolation, we might experience corrections, personal battles, testing, growth, and change. It is also a time of preparation and refinement. The wilderness is not meant to break us but transform us spiritually, emotionally, mentally, and physically. To grow, we must face trials, oppositions, and sometimes even ourselves.

What is the "wilderness"? The wilderness refers to the time when Jesus was led by the Spirit of God into the wild where he fasted for forty days and nights. This was also a time when he was tempted by the devil but overcame him. In the wilderness, Jesus was being refined, and as he was being refined, he was also being tested. During this period, Jesus was transforming into his full identity as the Son of God, ready to start his ministry that would change the world. Relating it to my life now, the pandemic has been like a wilderness for me, a long span of being separated from the world but intimate with God, to find my purpose and start living it.

In This Season

In this season, the tree stands alone
Its branches spread out
Some cracked and some old
While some of the leaves wither and die
Their time running out, their time to say goodbye

The tree stands alone
Not wanting to let go
Of the seasonal foliage that's lived out its time
The branches must drop
The leaves have to leave
And all the tree's clinging can't prevent what will be

The tree stands with new leaves and new branches
Lively and well, they come, and they go
The tree—
Roots will never go away
As time goes on
They will always be constant
They will always stay the same

Growth

....

"In this season" is about the season of separation, isolation, and restoration. I found myself throughout the years being separated from certain friends, family members, and lifestyles that did not fit the path that God was getting ready to put me on. This is not to say that I thought I was better than anyone; I have learned that people will have purpose in your life in different times for a variety of reasons, and only a few will stay with you throughout your life journey. In this season, I felt alone, but this isolation was necessary for my growth because God really worked on removing the branches (bad habits, traits, ways of thinking) that did not produce good fruit in my life. I know that when the time is right, He will bring the right friends and relationships into my life—friendships that are genuine, true, and mutually uplifting.

I Wait for You

Day and night I wait for you
Bones waxed cold
My soul longs for the assurances of the Lord
Dancing out of reach
My heart bursting with desires
Lingering at the tips of my dreams
Are the promises you spoke

Hope flooding my bloodstreams
Faith pulsing my veins
Expectation occupying my brain
I wait for you
Your blessings pouring out like rain
Watering my dry fields
Quenching my thirst
Buds start to bloom
Only at the right time
I continue to wait for you

A Season of Waiting

This whole "wilderness period" has also been a long season of waiting. Waiting on the visions, dreams, promises, and words spoken throughout my life. Waiting on my career to take off, on love to find me, my joy and peace to be more stable, and my calling in life to be clearer. I know waiting is unavoidable, it is a part of our journey in life, but it is the hardest thing to endure. God's timing is not our timing; there is an appointed time for everything, and no matter how much we try to force things to be, we cannot go ahead of time. Knowing this, I had to wait on God, which is something I was not used to doing. It is also important how we wait because it really works on our hearts and minds and positions us with our expectations to receive. In the waiting, I focused on pursuing my passions, advancing God's Kingdom, and bettering my character. Waiting also makes us humble because it allows us to focus on serving. I realized that during these past couple of years, I have been serving others more. Although waiting is very hard, it is necessary. As the saying goes, good things come to those who wait, and if you want the best, it will take time.

What They Think

Eyes piercing through skin
Leaving angry red lines
That don't seem to fade away
Their judgments burning
I'm scared of what they might say
Maybe their distain is all in my head
Maybe they just want to pity me instead
Maybe they don't care at all
Or maybe they are just waiting for me to fall
Nevertheless, I only care what you think

Internalized Failure

Caring too much about what others think about you steals your joy. I had put an invisible pressure on myself, which started to weigh me down. I started to worry about where I was at in life, instead of having peace in the present moment. I could not find a job after graduating during the pandemic in 2020, which became a continual struggle over the next two years. It was a struggle collectively, but I took it personally, as a sign of incompetency and failure. I was not afraid of what my family thought because they were supportive and understanding, but it was what I thought family-friends, acquaintances, and neighbours were thinking that concerned me. This stemmed from a family friend who would send me job alerts, and even an application at one point, suggesting that I go back to school. I cared so much about what people thought of me that I started to avoid them or conversations that would involve them asking me what I was doing. Being fearful of what others thought of me and the pressure I put on myself was pridefulness in disguise. I was not reaching the high standard that I set for myself, which did not give me any peace but allowed me to discover that not everything will go the way I planned, and that was okay. God has a way of showing us that we are not in control by disrupting our plans so that His original plan for us can be fulfilled. Just because your path is different does not mean you are lost. I had to start living for God and not for other people.

The Everlasting Well

Can you water these dry bones?
With milk and honey
I tried to find peace
But there isn't any
Trying and trying and trying again
To sooth my soul
And the thirst within me
I tried to find it in the world
But it's all temporary
Trying and trying and trying again
To fill this void
Can you hear me?

You answer . . .

Yes, I will water your dry bones
Not with milk and honey
But with the living water that is in all plenty
Because it will never run dry

True Satisfaction

Life is full of distractions, but I was at a point in my life where I could not use my busy schedule as an excuse to avoid the things inside that I did not want to face. Finishing school and being stuck in a lockdown brought me more time to reflect on what I wanted for my life. I was having a deep feeling of dissatisfaction, and I desired more of a relationship with God. There was a void in me that did not allow me to stay happy or satisfied, and I was tired of it. I thought a boyfriend, school, friends, travelling, moving to a new country, or getting a job could help lessen the feeling of emptiness, but it did not. Being in this world really made me lack peace because nothing could ever fully satisfy me. I could not find satisfaction in this world, so I decided to truly surrender my life fully to Christ and renew my faith, because the only way out of this dissatisfaction was Jesus. Christ says that he is the living water and the bread of life, whoever comes to him will always be satisfied, and that is a promise. We are all in need of life; some of us are living, but not truly living, we are empty shells within ourselves. We only truly come alive when we encounter Jesus. He says in John 4, he springs a well of everlasting (not temporary) life, love, and peace within us that will satisfy us and our every need. Jesus is that everlasting well that will never run dry.

Mount Zion

You sit high on Mount Zion
Looking over us
Climbing that great mountain
Cold earth underneath my palms
Rough rocks loosen my grip
Keep falling . . .
I get up, I try to reach you
But I am stuck
Wanting to give up
Your hands reaching out
Telling me to try again
To trust

Climbing that great mountain
Teary eyes turned upward

Reaching

A warm breeze embraces me
Just at my fingertips

Resistance

Feeling a constant strain, I was in a tug-a-war with my spirit and flesh. In the first couple of years of trying to get back right with God, I sensed an invisible resistance; no matter what I tried to do, I could not progress further. It seemed like I was taking twice the number of steps backwards than steps forward. This feeling did not go away, and it was not only with God but also my whole life, from the moment I graduated up until mid-2022. Despite my best efforts, my life felt stuck. My progression with Christ was not moving fast enough; instead, every little mistake made me feel like I was being pushed further away from God and my goals. I started to think that I was not good enough. This poem illustrates the frustration of not being able to go to a new level, spiritually and naturally, in life. It shows the desire to break forth to that mountaintop, the dwelling place with God. Life is not easy; there will be times where we stumble; but we have grace, which is something we cannot earn or even deserve. Grace is what helps us along our way; despite mistakes, we have a merciful and loving Father ready to help us. If we accept His help and trust Him along the way, we will surely make it up that mountain. For Psalm 37 says, "Though he falls, he shall not be utterly cast down: for the Lord upholds him with his right hand." So, to anyone else who has felt this way, I want to tell you to keep going because God's got you!

I Fall Short

I fall short of your glory
This fat is choking me
This flesh is killing me
Weighing me down
I cannot carry
My spirit shaking inside
Trying to break free
My eyes cannot see
My ears cannot hear
I cannot feel
Whenever you are near
Blind, I lean on my Faith
Deaf, I look to your signs
To guide me, to show me
That you're always there
Even though I fall short,
Short of your glory

Abounding Grace

For all have sinned and have fallen short of the glory of God
(Romans 3:23).

I faced so many corrections that it started to make me feel uncomfortable in my own skin. No matter what I did, it was like I always found a way to disappoint God. I associated my own disappointment with how I thought God was feeling about me. I did not give myself grace in the process of being worked on, which did not allow me to receive God's grace, either. I had to learn that it was out of love that we are corrected by God, just as how a loving parent would correct their child out of love for their own good. Correction done from a place of love is not something that we see a lot, because religion or the world will have you thinking that correction and love cannot co-exist. Many people are taught to think that if we do something bad, there is an angry God in Heaven waiting to condemn you and throw you into hell. This is not the case, God gives us many chances and time to get it right because He does not want to see any of us in hell, which was originally made for the enemy. However, that does not mean that we should abuse His love and grace, which gives us a new life outside of condemnation. Grace and love were God's way of effectively changing and working on our hearts and lives because love has a transforming effect and grace helps us to live transformed lives.

SIN

Chains slithering like snakes
Grabbing at her feet
Trying to bring her back into captivity
Enticing her with sin
Fighting so hard not to give in
But she does, as she does it again and again
Not wanting to abuse your grace
Knowing this was a cycle that needed to break
Feeling so ashamed

Like she couldn't escape
Then you reminded her your life is what it takes
To break those heavy restraints
Holding her in your arms, you tell her it's okay
Embracing you she releases her pain
That has burdened her with guilt and shame

You tell her not to hide away
Feeling so unworthy but wanting to change
Like the woman at the well
You do not hold her to her past
Like the adulterous woman
You do not hold her to her sin
Showing your tender mercies
You allowed her to live

Never casting the first stone

Mercy Endures Forever

For God did not send his Son into the world to condemn the
world, but to save the world through him
(John 3:17).

My poem "SIN" illustrates God's grace. There are two stories in the bible
of sinful women who were judged and condemned by their community, but
Jesus showed them mercy and kindness. The woman at the well went through
multiple men and was never satisfied, but Jesus showed up, showing her how
she could quench the thirst of her dissatisfaction. Despite the cultural differ-
ences, which did not permit them to speak to one another because she was a
Samaritan and Jesus was a Jew, Jesus did not care as he continued to talk to
her. Without judgment, Jesus told her everything about her life and told her
a way out, him. Similarly, Jesus did the same with the adulterous woman. She
was brought to him by religious leaders who were ready to stone her to death
because she was committing adultery, but Jesus challenged them. He told them
that the first without sin should cast the first stone; however, none of them
could and so they left, one by one. Jesus could have done it himself, because he
was without sin, but, instead, he showed her mercy and said to go and sin no
more. Although there is no follow-up to her story, I am sure this woman did
not go back and sin because of the unexpected mercy she received from Jesus,
which probably had a lasting effect on the way she lived her life from then on.
If we could grasp that love is everything and that it uplifts heavy burdens, casts
out fear, transforms us into better people, and most importantly saves us, then
I am sure we would live our lives differently.

An Epistle to God

Change me, oh Lord
Is what I look to you and pray
Warring against emotions
Each and every day
I wish my flesh would shrivel up
And fade away
Free from its heavy burden
Please do not delay
Give joy within my spirit
And please let it stay
I'm tired of being unhappy
I need this sadness to keep at bay
For when I am weak, you are my strength
So, hear me, oh Lord, when I say
I need you
I don't want to be the same
I beg, teach me to know your ways
My soul is cast down within me
Save me, oh Lord
My heart is dismayed
You tell me to find rest in you
So, in your peace, Lord, I will lay

A Believer's Prayer

....

During my own emotional turmoil, "An Epistle to God" is a believer's prayer I made, asking God to help me overcome struggles. We are in a constant battle between our flesh and Spirit, as Galatians 5:17 details in the bible, because the desire of the Spirit opposes the fleshy desires. These constant battles can cause distress and unrest in our lives. But, when we go before God and sincerely ask Him to help us and teach us His ways, He will give us rest from that constant tug-a-war. We become dead to the flesh and alive in the Spirit when we truly surrender to God, and it is not until we do so that we experience true freedom, peace, and joy. When we go to God, we find rest because He will uplift our hearts and give us strength to withstand temptation. The Word of the Lord says, "Let the weak say, 'I am strong'" (Joel 3:10). So, to anyone wrestling with their weaknesses, God says that in your weakness, He will strengthen you and make His power known. You are strong and an overcomer! When we give what we cannot control to God, we find peace during the struggle.

Haven

Take me to the place where the little cabin sits within a grassy meadow, with mountains all around, facing the sea. The crystal-white sand, beginning where the meadow ends, stretches forth into the cool water that beckons me from afar. I feel at peace here; unplugged, just me and You. I feel free here from my heavy burdens. I needed this. This is our meeting place, hidden from the rest of the world.

Healing Waters

Lord, let your healing water flow
Let it refresh and grow
The recesses of my mind
Like a sponge
Let it suck up negativity

Lord, let your healing water flow
Let it go down to my soul
Like a well-watered garden
Let it water these dry bones

Lord, let your healing water flow
Let it enter my heart
Soothing the aches and pains
Like a generator
Let it give me a fresh start

Lord, let your healing water flow
Let it fill up my womb
Like a never-ending spring, springing forth
Blessing every dysfunction
Let it birth something new

Lord, let it travel throughout my body
Let its remanence release
Healing, from every infirmity
And set me free
When your healing water flows

Ezekiel 37

In the valley of bones
The wind blows
Searching for a sign of life
On this scattered field of lost hope
Will you mend us back together—
Will you remove the stone?
Will you raise your people up again—
And have our hope restored?
Will you revive the pulses of our hearts—
Your Spirit, giving us a new start?
Will you breathe into these lungs of lead—
And resurrect everything that was once dead?

Making Lost Hope Come Alive

....

Bring living waters out of the desert places (Isaiah 41:18), turn my wilderness into greener pastures.

For a long part of my process, I have not seen the fruits of my efforts in finding a job and following my calling. During this time, I felt like I was just going through the motions, and I started to lose my motivation for life. Then, one day, I went to a young adults' service at church and a girl got up on stage and read Ezekiel 37. She started ministering about the dryness I was feeling, and how God would restore us, just as He did when He spoke life back into the dry bones in Ezekiel 37. The dry bones represented lost hope. It symbolized dreams, visions, and actual things in our lives that we have given up on because it felt like it was impossible to achieve. My dreams were like the scattered bones, and I needed someone to breathe life back into them; they needed to come alive again. This scripture encouraged me to dream again, so, I want to encourage anyone who is feeling hopeless to do the same. If you are going through a period of dryness in your life, in which you feel like there is no fruitfulness, do not give up, hold on. Every drought situation is about to be resurrected! In Ezekiel 37 the Lord prophesied to the dry bones, saying the hour has come where you will hear the voice of the Lord lifting you up from every grave situation and restoring your hope:

> And he said unto me, "Son of man, can these bones live?"
> And I answered, "O Lord God, thou knowest." Again he said
> unto me, "Prophesy upon these bones and say unto them, 'O
> ye dry bones, hear the word of the Lord. Thus saith the Lord
> God unto these bones; behold, I will cause breath to enter
> into you, and ye shall live'" (Ezekiel 37:3–5).

Abraham

Looking up to heaven
We were like those who dreamed
Counting all the stars
In darkness, I saw all the possibilities
Sprinkled across the night sky
Daring me to believe in the unseen
You called out saying
You will make nations out of me
Out of the loins of a man and the deadness of my womb
Springs forth the promises
My labour pains filling the air
In the stillness as I screamed
You birthed something new
That flower that was once a seed
Leaves behind a legacy

Look up at the Stars

Have you ever looked up at the broad sky and imagined all the possibilities about your future? Or have you ever had a vision or a dream that seemed so big, so amazing, so unreal, so far away? When I look at the story of Abraham, I am astonished by the faith he had in God's promise for a child despite the long wait. However, I am sure Abraham had his moments where it was hard to keep the faith on a promise that was taking a long time to come, which is probably why the Lord had to show him a vision in the stars. In Genesis 15:5, the Lord tells Abraham to "Look up at the sky and count the stars—if indeed you can count them ... So shall your offspring be." Sometimes, we need a vision to hold onto the plans God has spoken over our lives. And sometimes we just need a dream to convince us of the promise. Waiting for so long can make us so weary, to the point where whatever we are waiting for seems like it will never spring forth but will continue to be lifeless. However, there is a God that gives life to the dead and calls into being things that were not seen (Romans 4:17). Do not give up on your dreams.

OBEY YOU

My automatic response is to try and take control of everything
But you challenge me to let go of what I know
To surrender all control
To relax and trust you
Although it is so easy, it is not my natural course
Having that childlike faith
That a loving Father will take care of me
Even in the times that I must wait
I follow your commandments
Pursuing you with reckless abandonment
So, **YOUR** will, will be fulfilled
But it is hard because it is not **MY** natural will
My fleshly desires I struggled to kill
Yet, I know
You're working all things out for my good
Even though you cannot be understood
But I trust that you want better for me too
Choosing blessings over curses
I choose to obey you

If you fully obey the Lord your God and carefully follow all his commands I give you today, the Lord your God will set you high above all the nations on earth. All these blessings will come on you and accompany you if you obey the Lord your God: (Deuteronomy 28:1–2).

Chasing after the Wind (Ecclesiastes 1 & 2)

There is nothing new under the sun
This life is a song that has already been sung
Chasing after the wind
Like having faith without love
Meaningless
All things have been done
Moving towards the same fate
Fleeting, all things have an expiry date
Getting lost in the quickness of time
The work that has begun
Being passed down the line
As we toil aimlessly under the sun
Happiness without Him, the greatest pun
Only God's hand can change our outcome
What has been will be again
The truth is what King Solomon said
Emptiness, created from this life of sin
Meaningless
A chasing after the wind

What Is Life?

At one point, it hit me like a ton of bricks that life was meaningless without God. Questions flooded my mind: If I get what I want but do not have Jesus, will I truly be satisfied? Would I finally be contented with life? Is success worth it if I feel like I must keep chasing it and not enjoying the fruits of my labour? Like a never-ending cycle, many of us are chasing success. But, what is success? And, when do you know you have become successful? What does it profit me to gain this whole world and lose my soul (Matthew 16:26)? I realized it would profit me nothing. Therefore, I desired to know more about Jesus, because when we seek his Kingdom first, all other things will be added. True satisfaction is found in Christ, and when we find it in him, then we can enjoy the fruits of our labour and life will not be as meaningless. My desire is for my career to align with my calling in life, which is what I prayed to God about when I finished university in 2020. Little did I know that the struggles to find a stable job these past couple of years was God answering those prayers. I have seen many people stuck working in jobs they hated and missing out on pursuing their passions and dreams. We are taught that pursuing our passions does not grant us success, but that is wrong. Those passions are the things God has put in our hearts to pursue, and when we pursue what God is calling us to do, we will find success in it. It just takes patience, passion, consistency, discipline, and faith. We are created to live a life full of meaning.

Song of the Night

At night your song is with me
In quietness and solitude, I sit
Listening and revering at your glory
Not wanting it to end
Filling the atmosphere with your majesty
Darkness covering me as the streetlights shine in
Highlighting half my face while the rest stays hidden
Swaying in the stillness like magic
Not wanting to let go of our moment alone
I become one with the psalms
Lending my heart to the melody
Meditating on your words
Trying to find some form of remedy
As I stare at the sleepy world
I give into you
Blocking out the outside noise
Closely listening to the whisper of the wind
Revealing who I am in your faithful hymns
Secrets unravelling
My soul continues to sing

A Friend to Me

The night became a friend to me during this long phase of my life. I could not wait until the burst of colours of the dusk settled over the sky indicating the day was about to end. Then, it became dark, and if I were lucky enough, the stars would come out. I found comfort in the night; it was my cover from the world that seemed to never slow down during the day. It was my secret place, and a time to rest from the busyness. The night was where I was free to pour out my heart in songs. A place where I could dream and believe. The night was where I felt closer to heaven; it was where I belonged.

Praise You

In the darkest of nights, I will praise you
In my lonely hours, I will praise you
In the painful memories, I will praise you
In the midst of heartbreak, I will praise you
In the fountain of tears, I will praise you
When it's all not working out, I will praise you
When I don't see your promises yet, I will praise you
Even in the raging storm, I will still praise you
In the abundance of joy, I will praise you
In your peaceful presence, I will praise you
In the lovely moments, I will praise you
In all my blessings, I will praise you
In your morning light, I will praise you
When I'm at my strongest, I will praise you
When I'm at my healthiest, I will praise you
Even when you wrap me tight, I will still praise you

Praising in the Storm

It is easy to praise and believe in God when everything is good, but it is even greater when we continue to praise him in the bad times. Always Praising the Lord, no matter what, is true strength.

Solid Ground

Air has become my bed
Embracing me from beneath
Lungs feeling light
As it tries to escape my ribcage
I fall
Out of darkness into blue skies
Rippling like waves
Over your blinding figure
Riding through the sky
A black stallion
An angel reaches out, grabbing me before . . .
I fall
Finally, setting my feet on solid ground

Encounter in a Dream

I was falling in darkness, which was a dream I had before but would force myself out of it. However, this time, I allowed myself to fall until I fell into unexpected light. In the darkness, there was no direction or solid foundation. Similarly, this is what it was like without Christ because he is our firm foundation, the light of this world, and the way to everlasting life. We fall into darkness when we lose our way or do not even know it to begin with. Jesus came to earth, to set us free from the bondage of sin, to redeem us back unto God, and to restore the light of His glory. He is so merciful, because even when life seems to knock us off our feet, if we run to Jesus, he will set them on solid ground, as he called us out of captivity, to walk in freedom with him.

"In him was life, and that life was the light of all mankind. The light shines in the darkness, and the darkness has not overcome it" (John 1:4–5).

Hiding Place

Like a baby in its mother's womb, I rest in you
My hiding place
Protecting me, my safe refuge
I float in your warm presence
Covering me in your peace
Free, but tied to the umbilical cord
Feeding me with the word
Pumping life into my maturing body
I continue to grow in your love
Basking in your glory
Surrounded by your light
The days you have written for me
In your book of life
Close to my arrival
You call
You ordained me
For such a time as this

In His Presence

One morning, I had this overwhelming urge to just curl up and hide myself in the Lord like a baby in its mother's womb. I wanted to be sheltered from life and hidden in the peace of His presence. Away from my worries and the anxiety that came along with them, I needed that safe refuge to comfort and protect me. In Psalm 91:1–2, it says, "Whoever dwells in the shelter of the Most High will rest in the shadow of the Almighty. I will say of the Lord, 'He is my refuge and my strength, my God in whom I trust.'" I needed to let go, lean back, rest and take refuge in the Lord. When we try to take control of everything in our current situations, which are sometimes out of our control, it can cause us stress. But, the Lord tells us to retreat in Him. If you are feeling the overwhelming pressure of life right now, find rest in God. Abide in His presence. Let His peace cover you like a blanket, protecting your heart and mind. Most importantly, let His love overwhelm you, as you dwell in Him.

"You are my hiding place; you will protect me from trouble and surround me with songs of deliverance" (Psalm 32:7).

Found

Stars hang like chandeliers
Fog covers the moon
As breaths turn to smoke
Frost on your face
Melting snowflakes into an open palm
Standing deep in the White Sea
Sharp icicles hanging from leafless branches
Water dripping from its translucent skin
Elysium
A painted canvas of dark blues and greys
Orange and reds warming the sky
Green buds blooming into flowers
Disappearing in the tall grass
Like our cold time spent together
Petals being swept away
Getting lost in a dream

Ecclesiastes 3:1

....

"There is a time for everything, and a season for every activity under the heavens."

This is one of my favourite scriptures because there is a time for everything in our lives. This poem gives a detailed illustration of the seasons changing from a cold to a warmer time but is split apart by one word Elysium. Elysium means Paradise, representing heaven, because, as Ecclesiastes says, the season for every activity takes place under the heavens, here on earth. The coldness of winter depicts those instances when we might not feel the warmth of the Lord's joy but, instead, the absence of it. However, the warmth of spring shows a more beautiful scenery, in which things are just starting to bloom and spring forth. This time represents spiritual awakenings, new beginnings, and a sense of renewal and restoration. There will be some moments in our lives when we feel lost, but feelings, like the seasons, are temporary. What is important to know is that no matter what we might face or feel, we will always be FOUND in Christ.

Naked

I strip myself bare
As I come
Casting all my worries and cares
At the altar
Nothing else left
My life I give to you
Take away my worries of what people might think
Take away the anxiety of where my life should have been
And the longing love that I have for him
My fear of falling behind
Now wanting to fall back into sin
I'm choosing to trust you
Let your love comfort me
And your peace guard me from within
Let your joy strengthen me
And your encouraging words that I will win
I will make it
Losing my life to gain it
Vulnerable in my nakedness
I come bare to you

Armor

Put on your full armor
And let it shield you from the raging wind
Let it cover your head with salvation
And hide you from the wages of sin

Let it cover your chest
With the breastplate of righteousness
Protecting you from the arrows
Threatening to pierce through your skin

Put on your full armor
And let the word cut through the enemy's camp
Like a double-edge sword
Leaving on it Christ's stamp

Let it hold up your waist with the belt of truth
Concealing you with the most holy faith
Guiding you in His perfect peace

Leading a victory, you can almost taste

...

As the war continues to go on

Victory

Surrounded
I cry, "Open my eyes!"
To see past my enemies
That are advancing me
Aiming arrows of destruction
And spears of death
I cry, "Open my eyes!"
Deliver and set me free
From the grips of their hands
Paralyzing me in anguish
As my heart shrinks
Bounded by fear
I cry, "Open my eyes!" ...
Finally, answering me
You open them to let me see
The bigger army surrounding my enemies
And the shining armor on my body
Its light glaring in the dark field
I take out my shield
Quenching the fiery darts
Piercing into their hearts
With my angels behind me
Standing bold in Faith
I step forth into Victory

Bigger than Our Problems

And Elisha prayed, "Open his eyes, Lord, so that he may see." Then
the Lord opened the servant's eyes, and he looked and saw the hills
full of horses and chariots of fire all around Elisha
(2 King 6:17).

Why do we make our problems, or even the enemy, look bigger than they
are? We tend to glorify our fears, worries, and problems, but, as David said
in Psalms 56, when we are afraid, we must put our trust in the Lord. God is
bigger than our problems. By knowing this, we should not be fearful. However,
it can be hard to see that God is bigger when He is a Spirit, so instead, we focus
on the problem that has materialized in front of our eyes. Sometimes, we must
be like Elisha and ask the Lord to open our eyes, to see past our problems to
who is backing us up.

Rest

I sit at the feet of Jesus
Bringing peace to my weary soul
Pouring my heart out through my pain
Like Hannah kneeling before the Lord
Drunken by the state of sorrow

Running rivers filled the dry place
As you said, sing barren woman
And trust in the plans that I have made
For you will be a mother to many in the coming days
Rest and wait patiently for me

I am expanding you, extending your cords
Do not hold back or be afraid
Just trust in the Lord
The meek shall inherit the land
Because faithful I shall stand

Be still and see, your deliverance is near
Although you are weary
Do not give up
Your breakthrough is here

Right Where I Am Supposed to Be

I never thought of myself as an anxious person or one to worry a lot; however, for the last couple of years, I found myself having panic attacks and worrying about where my life was going. I had no peace, as I unconsciously built an altar of worry and tried to do multiple things to take control of my life. I wanted to speed up the process that God was taking me through. Frustrated, disappointed, and filled with pride, I became impatient. But, when I finally got tired of trying to do God's part and started to accept where I was at in my life, I entered a resting period. I was right where God wanted me to be, and a lot of people had been telling me this all along. I just needed to trust that God was working everything out for my own good, while preparing me for the next chapter.

I Choose Healing Instead

....

Curled up in a small ball on this large bed
You take it as an invitation to climb in
Lingering as you please
Covering me like a blanket
Following me like a shadow
You would not let me be
Sleep has become my escape
But not this time, I have decided to wake up and address you
Pain, I call to you, get out of my bed

Pain, you are not welcome here
I choose healing instead

Pain, you are not a part of me
I detach myself from you

Pain, I will no longer give you the right to hurt me
I am not yours to pursue
Pain, be silent,

Get out of my head
Pain, you are dead to me

I don't want to know you again

Pain to Purpose

You cannot talk about healing without talking about pain. I remember one night, a couple months ago, just feeling the weight of my own pain. It was like everything that I have ever stored up internally, in my heart, became external, and as I laid there, curled up on my bed, I felt paralyzed. I could not move or pray, while my pain became a living, breathing thing, pulsating throughout my body. I had never experienced anything like this before, but as I fell asleep, I felt it covering me like a blanket. Then, a few hours later, I woke up abruptly to a sharp physical pain in my arm. And do you know what was the first thought that came into my head? I deserved it. I deserved this pain. The next morning, I did not feel like myself, because I felt so far away from God. So, I put on some worship music and started praying, and while I did so the scripture Isaiah 53 came to me. This scripture talks about Jesus and how he took our pain and suffering by going on the cross. The punishment that brought us peace was on him. I heard a voice saying to me, "How can you say you deserve pain when he took it from you? If you deserve pain, then Jesus dying on the cross was for nothing."

The one who did not deserve any of the pain and suffering took it all from me. And why? Because of love. We still live in a world where suffering is inevitable, BUT, because of Jesus, we can have peace to overcome.

Changing my mindset from thinking I deserved pain, started a process of healing.

Redeemed

Come to me all who are weary
Broken down, weighted by chains
Creating deep wounds that bleed, trying to cover up the stains
I hear you—
Suffering in silence, your heart crying out for the one that saves

I am the burden bearer
Longing to lift those heavy loads leaving your shoulders weak with pain
I call to you to give it all to me
All your hurt and shame, as I set you free in Jesus' name
I am the great Physician
Specializing in putting back the pieces that fell apart
Healer of the scars you carry
And Mender of the broken hearts
Curing you from every sickness, affecting your mind, body, and soul
And from the past that has kept its hold
When you come to me, you will never be alone
I am that constant Friend you can confide in
The one standing with you in the middle of the storm
Wrapping you with my peace
Your comforter in the times where your grief runs deep

I am your Saviour
Breaking bondage from within
Grace abounding
My blood stronger than your sins
Holding you as my child
New life begins, as I reach from above
Turning darkness into light
Covering you with my love
I call to you to lay your burdens down
Come now to me, all who are weary . . .
And I will give you rest.

Come to me, all you who are weary and burdened, and I will give you rest. Take my yoke upon you and learn from me, for I am gentle and humble in heart, and you will find rest for your souls. For my yoke is easy and my burden is light (Matthew 11:28–30).

Transition

Break forth waters out of deserted land
Where it's dry and weary
Quench the thirst of my soul
Create rivers out of my swelling eyes
As tiny crystals leak
Capture it in your bottle for keepsake
Are they not in your book?
Lead me in the way I should go
Make the crooked path straight
You make a way out of no way
Order my steps
Guide me through this wilderness
A lantern at my feet
My heart you well keep
Bringing me to the other side
To my love where I will abide
Hidden, in your Holy Matrimony

In Between

The awkward "in between" is what I called a transition period; a period where you find yourself finished with one thing and in the process of moving forward into the next. The hardest and most significant transition in my life was the years after graduating university. Graduating university is what we would call "real life" kicking in: careers, family, and everything else in between. However, my career did not start right after, like I planned. My life was put on pause so that God could get my attention. Everything I experienced in this wilderness stage was preparing me and moving me towards my true passion, which is writing. In the wilderness, we can be still from the distractions of our busy lives and re-focus on God and the plans He has for us.

We have ideas, inventions, books, and songs that are deep within us, but we need that time alone, with no distractions, to discover and bring them out. The promises and stories of our lives are already written out; we were not meant to live a life of mediocracy. God is not conventional; His ways are not our ways. Once we accept that and trust Him, then we can enjoy the process of our life journey and the adventures it has along the way.

Peace

Come, rest in me, my child
I will lift those heavy burdens
And mend your broken heart

Come, rest in me, my child
I will wipe away your tears
And take away the pain

Come, rest in me, my child
I will uplift your spirit
And let all your worries be swept away

Come, rest in me, my child
I will be your shelter from the storm
And give you peace in the middle of the night

Come, rest in me, my child
I will be your hiding place

Come, rest in me, my child
And just let me love you

Promise Land

My tears have become my food
And the pillow beneath my head
Keeping me up at night
A running stream I sowed in
And began to grow

In the midst of sorrow, I planted my seed
In the place that felt forgotten
There, it started to turn green
Light shining through the darkness
I started to see

My days have come
My mourning turned to dance
My tears to laughter
My pain to peace
Under the open heavens
You finally came to me . . .
. . . My harvest of joy

At the break of dawn
You fought for me

Now the lines have fallen in pleasant places
My inheritance, you are secured
Underneath the open heavens
Crossing over, my freedom is ensured
As I finally enter the land you've promised

Beautiful in Its Time

Teetering on the edge of solid ground and the abyss
I plead to you
Do not let me go back in the darkness
Fighting to stay but close to falling
Weakened by the weight of gravity pulling me forward
I repeat
Your joy is my strength, your joy is my strength

"Just hold on a little longer
"The rainbow is coming," you said
But, I can't see through this mist
This rainstorm is blinding
Drenching my clothes, heavy, pulling me down further

Suddenly, I catch your wind blowing me upwards
A hand pulling me in
"Fall back and rest"
You tell me to trust you
In a trembled voice, I said
"I am trying"
My tears making pools in the palm of your hands

"I am scared to fall"
A light whisper to my ears
"I will catch you"
"Don't be afraid; I am with you"
Letting it all go
My life in your hands

I fall into a soft cloud
Your light piercing through
Arch of colours glistening under the sun
Above the rainstorm into the clear blue
Red, blue, purple, yellow

Not one of them the same
But, now I finally see
Through this journey of pain
You make everything beautiful in its time

Moving Towards the Grander Picture

We must learn to accept the process. It was hard for me to because I could not see the steps ahead and going through a process can be challenging. I used to be fearful about the outcome of my future and if I would do everything that God has planned for me, but I realized that I needed to have faith in the process of my life. We need to have faith that everything is working out for our own good, even when we cannot see it because all our experiences, good and bad, are what makes up our stories. That story can be beautiful, but it is only when we trust and commit our lives to Christ. We cannot give up but believe in the promises of God, even in the darkest moments, and rejoice in those dark moments, as we hold onto hope. Only God sees the bigger picture of our lives. It is up to us to step in faith and trust that our stories will unravel into something beautiful. We cannot see the purpose in the pain, but God prepares us through our experiences for the greater things He has for us who believe. We must hold on a little longer. We are called to live by faith and not by sight, to not be discouraged in what we do not see, but to be encouraged in what we can see through our imagination and the Word of God. It takes faith to see past the storm clouds to the blue skies ahead. In Jeremiah 29:11 it says, the Lord's plans are to prosper us not harm us, and to give us hope and a future.

Freedom

Freedom is the wind blowing against our outstretched arms, waving out of the car window as we drive down an open road

It's the branches hanging low, making an alcove in the nature surrounding us

It is the feeling of flying we get as we imagine touching the sky and the tranquility we feel when no one else is around

Freedom is the inner peace guarding my heart and mind, surpassing all understanding that would try and take it away from me

It's dancing underneath the night sky as the stars stand as audience to my worship

It's the never-ending love that breaks chains, sets us free from fear, and makes us stand tall

Freedom is the confidence knowing that, even if we fall, we will rise again

True Freedom

This marks the end of my book but not the end of my story. I wanted to end with this poem called "Freedom" because it embodies what being a follower of Christ is, which is to be free. In this world, we have a false sense of freedom. There are so many people bounded by chains—mentally, emotionally, spiritually, and physically. So many people are suffering mentally and emotionally from illnesses such as depression. And physical bondage like health, finances, family, cultural setting, demographics, and (or) governmental pressures, which can weigh us down. We can also feel spiritual bounded by the way we are living, which can keep us from truly connecting with our Creator. God sent Jesus to die for our sins, so that we can be free from the chains of this world.

I am hoping that through this collection of poetry and prose, you were able to see another side of Jesus that you might have not seen. To see him as a saviour, friend, healer of the broken-hearted, refuge/safe place, the prince of peace, and to see God as a Father. A Father who will meet you at your urgent need in the middle of life's storm. It is only in Him that we are guaranteed a better hope for our future because in Jesus we receive life abundantly. I pray that you will let Christ in, as he knocks at the door of your heart. John 16:33 says, "I have told you these things, so that in me you may have peace. In this world you will have trouble. But take heart! I have overcome the world."

About the Author

Star Antoinette is an up-and-coming Canadian poet and writer who explores how life experiences work within a greater purpose. In her pursuit of fulfilling her passion for writing, she did a bachelor's specialization in English Literature at the University of Ottawa. She has her own ghostwriting business called Starlight and a podcast called *Finding Faith, Finding Me*, which helps others to find their identity and walk in their God-given purpose. Navigating her own battles in her journey of faith, Star is a mental health advocate and has her certificate in Safe Talk for suicide prevention. When she is not writing, she is travelling or spending time with her family. *Beautiful in its Time; Finding My True Identity*, is Star's first published book.

Printed in the USA
CPSIA information can be obtained
at www.ICGtesting.com
LVHW011141211123
764515LV00013B/643/J

9 781039 174948